HEINEMANN STATE STUDIES

Michigan
Native Peoples

Marcia Schonberg

Heinemann Library
Chicago, Illinois

© 2004 Heinemann Library
a division of Reed Elsevier Inc.
Chicago, Illinois

Customer Service 888-454-2279

Visit our website at www.heinemannlibrary.com

Designed by Heinemann Library
Photo research by Stephanie L. Miller and Kathy
    Creech
Maps by Kimberly Saar/Heinemann Library
Printed in the United States by Lake Book
    Manufacturing, Inc.

08 07 06 05 04
10 9 8 7 6 5 4 3 2 1

**Library of Congress
Cataloging-in-Publication Data**
Schonberg, Marcia.
   Michigan native peoples / Marcia Schonberg.
     p. cm. -- (Heinemann state studies)
Summary: Discusses the traditions, clothing, food,
tools, and current status of the different tribes of
Native Americans who made their home in what
became the state of Michigan. Includes biblio-
graphical references and index.
   ISBN 1-4034-0660-X (Hardback) -- ISBN 1-4034-
2678-3 (pbk) 1. Indians of North America--Michi-
gan--History--Juvenile literature. 2. Indians of
North America--Michigan--Social life and customs--
Juvenile literature. [1. Indians of North America--
Michigan.]
I. Title. II. Series.
E78.M6S36 2003
977.4004'97--dc22
                                    2003016130

Acknowledgments
The author and publishers are grateful to the
following for permission to reproduce copyright
material:
Title page (L-R) Jeff Foott/Bruce Coleman, Inc., Mar-
tin Reinhardt, Courtesy of the Northern Indiana Cen-
ter for History; contents page (L-R) John Flesher/AP
Wide World Photo, David Carrigan; p. 6 David Carri-
gan; p. 7 Carl & Ann Purcell/Corbis; p. 8 Daniel C.
Fisher/Museum of Palentology/The University of
Michigan; p. 9 Jeff Foott/Bruce Coleman, Inc.; p. 10
Exhibit Museum of Natural History/The University of
Michigan; pp. 11, 13 Marilyn "Angel" Wynn/Native-
Stock.com; pp. 12, 26, 27 Hulton Archive/Getty
Images; p. 14 State Archives of Michigan; pp. 16, 21
Bettmann/Corbis; pp. 17, 23, 24, 29 Corbis; pp. 18,
19, 22 North Wind Picture Archives; p. 20 The New-
berry Library; p. 28 Geoffrey Clements/Corbis; p. 30
Old World Auctions/oldmaps.com; pp. 31, 33, 34
The Granger Collection, New York; p. 32 The Ohio
Historical Society; p. 35 Courtesy of the Northern
Indiana Center for History; p. 36 John Flesher/AP
Wide World Photo; pp. 40, 41 Martin Reinhardt

Cover photographs by (top, L-R) Jeff Foott/Bruce
Coleman, Inc., The Granger Collection, New York,
Robert Lifson/Heinemann Library, The Granger Col-
lection, New York; (main) Macduff Everton/Corbis

The publisher would like to thank expert reader
Martin Reinhardt, director of the Center for Native
American Studies, Northern Michigan University.

Special thanks to Alexandra Fix and Bernice Anne
Houseward for their curriculum guidance.

Some words are shown in bold, **like this.** You
can find out what they mean by looking in the
glossary.

Contents

First Peoples

When we study history, it is important to remember that what we learn is based on many points of view. History is not usually recorded as it happens. What is written as history can be based on how different people saw an event. Many times, this perception is not the same from person to person.

When studying Native Americans, there is a lot of information that has been **interpreted** by scientists and **archaeologists.** Their interpretations may not be accurate. Also, much of Native American history was passed down orally. It was not written down. History was told through stories that could change each time the story was retold. As a result, the true facts of what happened may not be what we read in a book today.

Migration Routes

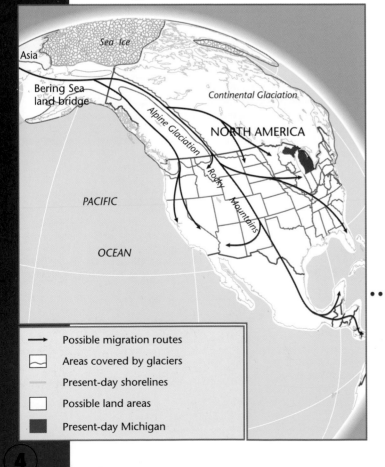

Asia

Sea Ice

Bering Sea land bridge

Continental Glaciation

Alpine Glaciation

NORTH AMERICA

Rocky Mountains

PACIFIC

OCEAN

→ Possible migration routes

Areas covered by glaciers

Present-day shorelines

Possible land areas

Present-day Michigan

THE BEGINNING

The history of how Native Americans came to the area that is now North America is different depending on who is telling the story. For example, some scientists believe the first people to live on the land we call

Most Native Americans believe their people have always been in the Americas. Evidence suggests that Paleo-Indians probably came from Asia, across a land bridge.

Michigan today arrived between 12,000 and 20,000 years ago, following the last **Ice Age.** These people were **nomadic** hunters. They created weapons from stone and hunted **mammoths, mastodons,** and other large animals. The animals moved across the land in search of food. The nomads followed these animals as they moved. The hunters preserved the animal meat in frozen lakes and used other parts, like the tusks and fur, for shelter. The animal skin or hide was used for clothing.

An Ancient Discovery

Scientists often uncover the past by accident. In the 1990s, Harry Brennan, who lived near Saline, Michigan, decided to build a pond on his land. During the digging process, workers discovered buried mastodon bones. Even more astounding, Dr. Dan Fisher from the University of Michigan found mastodon tracks buried beneath Mr. Brennan's land. These discoveries are thought to be about 11,000 years old. A reproduction of the Mastodon Trackway is on display in the University of Michigan's Museum of Natural History in Ann Arbor.

According to scientists, these nomads began their journey in Asia as the Ice Age ended and **climate** temperatures began warming. It is believed they walked across a land bridge called Beringia that connected the **continents** of Asia and North America. Today, land no longer connects these two continents. Beringia is now covered by the Bering Sea.

Some native peoples tell a different story about how the Earth came to be, with their people living on it. The Ojibway, a tribe with members that live in Michigan, share a story of how a great flood left the Earth with no land for the animals to stand on. Only Nanaboozhoo, the **cultural** hero of the Anishinaabek, and a few animals who were able to swim or fly survived. To try to recreate the Earth, Nanaboozhoo decided to swim to the bottom of the ocean to grab a handful of the Earth. He believed that with that bit of land, they could create a new Earth for themselves with the help of their Creator.

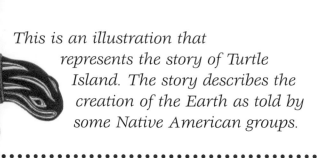

This is an illustration that represents the story of Turtle Island. The story describes the creation of the Earth as told by some Native American groups.

Several animals also took turns trying to reach the bottom of the ocean, but failed. The muskrat was finally able to grab a handful of Earth from the bottom of the ocean, but died after running out of air. However, when it floated to the surface, Nanaboozhoo saw the Earth was still clenched in the muskrat's hand. The turtle told Nanaboozhoo to place the Earth on his back so it could grow. The winds began to blow, and the little piece of Earth on the back of the turtle grew larger and larger. Soon it was an island in the water, and the animals had land to stand on. This became known as Turtle Island, or what we call North America today. Not long after, with the help of the Creator, people appeared on Earth as well.

Paleo-Indians: 13,000 to 7,000 b.c.e.

The early people who arrived on foot or in small canoes left untold stories. **Archaeologists** have pieced together their history by searching for clues in the tools, weapons, and art objects left behind. Skeletons and evidence of communities that are unearthed help scientists tell the mysterious tales of these **prehistoric** residents. They are called the Paleo-Indians by scientists and some historians, and are considered Michigan's earliest people.

Archaic Indians: 8,000 to 500 b.c.e.

Archaeologists called the next group of inhabitants the Archaic Indians. These people were most likely related

Archaeologists have learned that during the time of Michigan's early peoples, atlatls were used all over the world.

to the Paleo-Indians, but **climate** changes forced them to live their lives differently from their **ancestors.** The Archaic people had more advanced tools than the Paleo-Indians. The Archaic Indians introduced the atlatl, a wooden spear thrower that made their pointed darts fly on target. The Archaic Indians used it to hunt smaller animals they found in the forests. They also developed a common language called **Algonquian** by some. However, each tribe had unique words, so tribes from different places often had difficulty understanding each other.

One group of Archaic Indians, named the Old Copper Indians by scientists, lived on Isle Royale, an island in northern Lake Superior. This **archaic** tribe was one of the first to use metal in many ways. They mined copper for their weapons and **artifacts. Remnants** of their old copper mines are still on the island. These people buried their relatives in cemeteries and they farmed. Scientists say the Old Copper Indians may have invented the birch bark canoe used by many later tribes.

THE WOODLAND COMMUNITIES: 500 B.C.E. TO C.E. 500

The Archaic period ended about 500 B.C.E. The Woodland **Cultures** were the next group of people who most

*Scientists believe the **mastodon** tracks found in Saline were left by a large male mastodon that was about nine feet tall at the shoulder and weighed approximately six tons.*

likely **descended** from the Archaic Indian tribes. The first of the Woodland **Cultures** were the Adena tribes. These people used farming as a means of getting food and learned to trade with other groups. They also built mounds from earth, so **archaeologists** called them moundbuilders. These mounds were believed to be used for cemeteries and ceremonies. Historians say the largest of these mounds was along the Rouge River, close to the Detroit River. Early settlers measured it at 400 hundred feet wide, nearly 800 feet long, and 40 feet tall. It no longer exists today. Many historical mounds were destroyed as cities and towns were built where native peoples once lived.

THE HOPEWELLS

The Hopewell Indians, one of the Middle Woodland tribes, lived from about 100 B.C.E. to C.E. 500. Like the Adena Indians who came before them, mounds were also important to this tribe and they were also called moundbuilders. They may have used the mounds for ceremonies, burials, and as sundials to tell the seasons. By placing their mounds to cast shadows from the sun, they were able to keep track of the seasons and time. They built dirt mounds covered with stones and grass along the Saginaw River and near many other rivers including the Detroit, Grand, and Rouge Rivers in Michigan's Lower Peninsula. Norton Mounds near the present day city of Grand Rapids represent one of their famous burial mounds.

Although artifacts dug up by archaeologists provide great clues to how native peoples of the past lived, many people, including Native American tribes, believe it is wrong to disturb the burial grounds of their **ancestors.**

In the 1900s, archaeologists found pottery containers, ceremonial objects, and smoking pipes that were shaped like animals. These items were decorated with shells and gems from areas far from Michigan. Based on these **artifacts,** scientists believe these ancient peoples traded with other tribes living as far away as the Rocky Mountains and the Gulf of Mexico, where these gemstones and shells were plentiful.

Some of the Hopewell's drawings were carved into stone. They used simple stone carving blades to make **petroglyphs.** Thousands of years later, these pictures remain, but so many years of exposure to weather—ice, snow, rain, and sun—has faded them. It is believed they could be more than 1,000 years old. The faint rock carvings of animals at the Sanilac Petroglyphs are visible today. They are located in eastern Michigan, near Cass City.

The quarter placed beneath the petroglyph gives you an idea of the size of the drawings.

Three Fires Confederacy

Many different tribes, **clans,** and bands of native peoples have a history that includes the land now known as Michigan, but three tribes are especially well known throughout the state. These people called themselves the "Anishinaabek," or "the first people." Their **ancestors** were the Late Woodland people—the last of the **prehistoric** tribes. They each speak Anishinaabemowin, an **Algonquian** language similar to the language spoken long ago by their ancestors. It is believed that they **migrated** to the Great Lakes region before European explorers came to the area.

Corn was the most important crop of the Potawatomi, but they also farmed squash, beans, and pumpkins.

The Anishinaabek call themselves the Three Fires Confederacy. They also call each other "the three brothers." The three tribes are the Ojibway (Chippewa), Ottawa (Odawa), and Potawatomi (Bodwewadomi). The Ottawa and Potawatomi sometimes call the Ojibway "older brother." The Ottawa are next, and the Potawatomi are the "younger brother."

Food

Long ago, thc Anishinaabek relied mostly on **foraging** as a way to find the food they needed to survive. Men and women were both responsible for getting food. The men and boys usually did the hunting and fishing while the women and girls gathered and prepared plants for food.

What groups did to get food depended on where they lived. There were four **subsistence** patterns in the Great Lakes area. These patterns were based on **agriculture,** large **game** hunting, rice, and fishing.

Native American tribes in southern Michigan grew corn, beans, and squash because of the **climate.** The area had at least 120 frost-free growing days, and 140 growing days were needed for growing corn. The people living here also hunted, fished, and collected wild plant foods. Deer, bison, turkeys, elk, bears, and other animals were sources of meat. Further north where it was colder, they depended on moose, caribou, and bears for food. Beaver, rabbits, large birds, and fish were eaten as well. West of

Wigwams were usually built in less than a day. They were only used for sleeping, storing goods, and escaping from bad weather.

Lake Michigan, Native Americans developed an **economy** based on wild rice. People living in the Upper Peninsula near Lakes Michigan, Huron, and Superior depended very heavily on fishing for their food because the **climate** was not good for growing crops. Because the groups of Michigan had different foods available to them, much trade occurred during seasonal gatherings.

HOUSING

Until the 1800s, the primary housing for the Anishinaabek were dome-shaped wigwams. Poles used to support the structure were placed in the ground, bent, and tied to achieve shape. The cross lodge poles are placed so they create the design of a medicine wheel in the center of the roof of the structure. The walls were covered with birch, cedar, or elm bark. In the summer, woven mats made from reeds and grasses found in the swampy areas near the lake were used in place of the bottom row of bark to allow more air into the wigwam. The women would weave the materials together with a shaped bone needle. These sturdy mats or cedar tree branches were used to cover the earthen floors. The doorway of the wigwam always faced east toward the rising sun, and it was usually covered by an animal skin.

COMMON BELIEFS

The Three Fires tribes share a basic belief system. They believe in the spiritual connection of all things in the world. The stories they pass down to their children

Medicine Wheels

The medicine wheel is a spiritual symbol common to many native tribes, including the Anishinaabek. Each part of the Anishinaabek medicine wheel has a specific meaning. It is a circle divided into four parts that correspond to four directions. The circle represents all of Creation. The lines represent the circles of life and **humanity.** The crossing of the lines represent balance and harmony. Eagle feathers are often attached and represent the connection between people and the Creator. Medicine wheels often have four colors—yellow, red, black, and white—that represent the four cardinal directions of east, south, west, and north. The Anishinaabek are taught that everything begins in the east, just like the new day.

teach about the "Great Spirit," or the Creator, called Gitchie Manitou. The Creator gave each of the Three Fires tribes the special task described by their names. The Ojibway are the "keepers of the faith." The Ottawa are the "trader people," and the Potawatomi are the "keepers of the fire."

There are many traditional oral stories are handed down through generations of Anishinaabek. They are often based on history, and always contain teachings about how to live properly according to tribal tradition. Some stories are long and others are short. One tells of how the Potawatomi, Ottawa, and Ojibway people became one tribe. Another is the story of how corn originated. The Anishinaabek are also taught about the medicine wheel.

DODEMS

The Anishinaabek are traditionally governed by a **clan** system. The members of a clan are dependent upon one another. All members are considered one—if one member is hurt, they all are hurt. They do not have one main tribal chief. Each **clan** has its own leadership.

Chief Okemos

Chief Okemos, the nephew of Chief Pontiac, lived near present-day Mason and Okemos, Michigan. He was given the title of *ogemaa*, or chief, of the Ojibway because of his courage. He was badly wounded when his tribe sided with the British in battle against American troops. After the war, Chief Okemos signed a **treaty** with Lewis Cass, the territorial governor of Michigan. Today, students who attend Central Elementary School in Okemos, Michigan, know about their school marker that reads: "Erected in memory of Chief Okemos, whose tribe once occupied the grounds upon which this school stands. Brave in battle, wise in council, honorable in peace."

Traditionally, the clan, or dodem, is **inherited** through the father's **ancestors.** Today, because of **mixed-ancestry,** some inherit their dodem from their mother's father. Anishinaabek are not supposed to marry within their own clan.

THE OJIBWAY

There are several spellings for the name of this tribe. Ojibway, Ojibwa, and Ojibwe are the most common. French explorers mistakenly called the Ojibway tribe the "Chippewa," a name that is still used by some today. There are several **interpretations** of the word "Ojibway." Some believe it means something like "to roast 'til puckered," describing the way the top of their **moccasins** looked. Others say it refers to the practice of recording information by drawing pictures and signs on birch bark. These people lived close to Lake Superior and along the western shores of Lake Huron. They had a large fishing village at the rapids of the St. Mary's River, which is now Sault Ste. Marie.

The Ojibway follow the teachings of the Seven Grandfathers. The story of the Seven Grandfathers says that each grandfather gave a gift to a chosen boy to bring back to his people. The seven gifts were wisdom, love, respect, bravery, honesty, **humility,** and truth. The boy grew into an old man before he was able to return home. When the man finally brought the gifts to his people, he explained the dangers that came with each and how each gift had an opposite that caused evil. The man also explained how in order to be healthy, people had to develop themselves both physically and spiritually. This could be done through fasting, dreaming, and meditation.

THE OTTAWA

The Ottawa, fulfilling the duties of their name meaning "to trade," traveled far to trade with the other tribes in the Great Lakes region, but made their home mostly along Lake Michigan. They traded furs, skins, corn, sunflower oil, tobacco, roots, and herbs with Native American tribes in the area, and later with European settlers as well. The Ottawa were also well known for their excellent birch bark canoes that assisted them in their travels.

The Ottawa were skilled hunters and fishers, although during the harsh winter months, they sometimes had to eat tree bark to survive. Women gathered nuts and berries and tapped maple trees for syrup.

Chief Matchekewis

Another Michigan Native American leader was Ojibway chief Matchekewis. He was one of the signers of the Treaty of Greenville in 1795. This treaty allowed the United States to occupy the traditional homelands of many different native peoples. It also provided peace and friendship between nations as well as protection of Indian tribes by the federal government. His signature allowed the U.S. to occupy Ojibway land including Bois Blanc Island in Lake Huron. Chief Matchekewis also participated in Pontiac's Rebellion during the take over of **Fort** Michilimackinac in 1763.

THE POTAWATOMI

The Potawatomi **migrated** to the Lower Peninsula, along the St. Joseph River, and further southwest into Indiana. They believe Gitchie Manitou made them responsible for keeping the Three Fire Tribes together as a family. For this reason, the Potawatomi are called "The People of the Place of Fire" and the "Keepers of the Sacred Fire."

Pontiac

One of Michigan's famous Ottawa leaders was Pontiac. He was born around 1720 near Detroit. Pontiac became an *ogemaa,* or chief, because he was a skillful speaker and leader. He believed that native peoples were suffering because they were no longer following their traditions and instead were following the ways of the European settlers. After siding with the French, and being defeated by the British during the French and Indian War, he encouraged nearby tribes to overthrow the British **forts.** Convincing other Native American leaders to join his uprising, they overpowered many of the forts they attacked. These battles were called Pontiac's Rebellion. They began in 1763 and lasted until 1766 when Pontiac, who incorrectly thought the French who remained in Michigan would help the Native American forces, was defeated at Fort Detroit. He left for Illinois where he was killed by a fellow warrior. Today, several places in Michigan, such as the city of Pontiac, are named for the famous chief.

Other Tribes of Michigan

The Three Fires tribes were not the only native peoples in the Michigan Territory. Six other tribes lived nearby. Five of them also used **Algonquian** languages. They were the Menominee, Sauk, Fox, Miami, and Kickapoo. These tribes moved often, looking for better hunting or farming locations. Sometimes they were forced from their land by other tribes. They moved to lands surrounding Michigan and when those became crowded, they moved back to Michigan.

THE MENOMINEE

The Menominee were an unusual tribe because they did not migrate from one area to another. They settled in the Upper Peninsula, near the Menominee River. They also call themselves Anishinaabek, but they are not part of the Three Fires Confederacy. This tribe speaks Anishinaabemowin, but it is a different **dialect** from the other tribes. Today, members of this tribe live mostly in Wisconsin.

The blackish wild rice grain the Menominee gather is used in soups, stews, and even pudding. Sometimes it is served with maple syrup.

Menominee people lived in villages of wigwams during the winter months while they were out hunting.

Living near the river has always been of great importance to the survival of the Menominee. The river provides fish and wild rice to eat. The tribe's dependence on wild rice provided the name for the tribe. The Anishinaabemowin name for rice is *manomin.* The Menominee are "the people of the rice."

Traditionally, the Menominee relied on hunting and gathered food resources, but they also maintained small gardens of corn, beans, and squash. They also fished a lot, especially for sturgeon. For this work, they used dugout and birch bark canoes. Women collected a wide variety of wild plant foods, including berries, nuts, roots, and wild greens. Hunting was done mostly by individuals or in small groups using bows and arrows, although they occasionally organized larger hunts for deer and buffalo. According to Menominee oral tradition, humans were **descended** from bears, so respect was paid to bears as well as to other animals.

The Menominee practiced their religious teachings continuously throughout the day. Like the Ojibway, they consider the number four to be sacred. Several times a year, usually before the changing season, they hold special celebrations. Life cycle events, like welcoming the birth of a baby, reaching **maturity,** marriage, and death, are cause for celebrations. Modern day native peoples often keep both their own traditions and as well as practice **Christianity** as introduced by the European settlers.

Sauk and Fox

The Sauk and the Fox are so closely associated that these two distinct tribes are usually considered to have been a single tribe. Although joined in very close alliance after 1734, the Sauk and Fox maintained separate traditions and chiefs. This was very apparent when Sauk and Fox chiefs were forced by the government to sign the same **treaty.** However, the signatures always appear in two distinct groupings, one for each tribe.

The Sauk call themselves *asa-ki-waki*, which means "people of the outlet" in their **Algonquian** language. The "outlet" they are referring to is the Saginaw River. This is where they first gathered as a people in the 1700s. They are also sometimes referred to as "people of the yellow earth." The Sauk women grew crops, including "the three sisters," and the men hunted. The men also traded for blankets, **ammunition,** guns, and knives.

The people called Fox call themselves Mesquakie. They were named Fox by French explorers in the 1600s. Mesquakie means "Red Earth People." The women raised crops and gathered food such as nuts, berries, and

The Sauk and Fox tribes believe that the Great Spirit chose their homelands and commanded them to live as brothers.

honey. The women were also responsible for raising children, maintaining their homes, and **tanning** hides. Men hunted deer and other animals with fur for food, clothing, and trading. They also made canoes. After horses were introduced in the 1700s, Fox men also made saddles and tended horses.

MIAMI

The Miami Indians lived around the Great Lakes, including an area in southwestern Michigan, near Illinois and Indiana. They were ruled by a **clan** system. Each Miami belonged to his or her father's clan. Clan chiefs in each village made up a council that governed the community.

The Miami lived in dome-shaped wigwams. Their villages were surrounded by large fields of corn. The Miami were famous for their excellent corn crops. They also grew melons, squash, beans, and pumpkins. Once a year, they went on buffalo hunts. During the 1700s, the Miami **migrated** from Michigan to Ohio.

KICKAPOO

The Kickapoo lived in eastern Michigan, with the Sauk and Fox tribes. They lived in villages during the warmer months as they grew corn, beans, and squash, and

Native Americans had over fifty uses for buffalo besides as meat for eating. They used buffalo to make teepees and clothes, water cups and spoons, and even fishing line.

gathered nuts and berries. Their homes were longhouses and had a smoke hole in the roof. During the colder months, the Kickapoo were **nomadic,** searching for animals to hunt for food. The Kickapoo were driven from Michigan by the Iroquois and Sioux tribes by the mid-1600s.

HURON

A sixth group, the Hurons, were an Iroquoian tribe. They spoke a different language from the other five tribes in Michigan. The Huron lived along Lake Huron, Lake Erie, Lake Ontario, and into Canada. They were the largest tribe in the Great Lakes region.

The Huron were sometimes considered by scientists as the most advanced Native Americans living in the Great Lakes area. The women were excellent gardeners and the men fished in nearby lakes and streams. The Huron Indians were known as skilled fur traders. Although related to the Iroquois in their beliefs and customs, the Huron competed with the other powerful Iroquois tribes that also traded furs. The competition between the groups resulted in the Huron being run off their land. Huron tribe members were also killed by diseases brought by European **missionaries.**

The Huron were also called Wyandot, a variation of their traditional name, Wendat. This name means "dwellers of the peninsula."

European Influence

French explorers were the first European people to arrive in the Great Lakes, around 1620. When these Europeans came to the area now known as Michigan, they kept travel journals. Writing about the native peoples they met was difficult, so different spellings and pronunciations of names and places occurred. Even so, their records explained what they found when they explored the land of the Great Lakes region.

Compared to other areas of the country, the native peoples of Michigan and the French explorers had few problems over land. The French explorers and settlers

This is an illustration of Native Americans and French traders dancing at a meeting in the forest.

British explorers were not pleased by the friendship between the French explorers and Native Americans.

relied on Native American people for help in learning to survive in forested Michigan. The native peoples shared their knowledge of the wilderness. They taught the Europeans canoe building, farming, and cooking methods. The Europeans learned how to live in the wilderness.

The French introduced their way of life—tools, alcohol, cooking pots, woolen clothes, guns, and **ammunition**—to Native American people. They offered these items and more in exchange for furs to take back to France. Once Native Americans tried these products, they were eager to bring **pelts** to the trading posts to trade. They also traded deer, raccoon, bear, wolf, and other animal pelts, but the French liked beaver pelts the most. Back home in France, beaver hats were popular and sold at high prices. The French set up their largest trading post where St. Ignacc is today, along the Straits of Mackinac.

Many of the explorers who first met the Native People were also French **missionaries.** They traveled from present-day Canada, along the St. Lawrence River. Originally, they hoped to find a new route to Asia. Instead, they claimed the land they found for France and tried to spread their **Christian** beliefs among the native peoples. The **forts,** missions, and trading posts became the center of French life among the native peoples.

Jacques Marquette and Louis Jolliet

In June of 1673, Louis Jolliet and Father Jacques Marquette set out on an **expedition** to explore the upper Mississippi River. They led French explorers on a journey that they hoped would lead to the Pacific Ocean. However, as they went further along the river, they realized it was flowing south to the Gulf of Mexico, and not west to the Pacific Ocean. Yet they pushed on until almost the mouth of the Arkansas. Here the Indians told them that the gulf was only ten days away, but also that **hostile** Indians would be found along the way. The explorers also noticed the presence of Spanish trade goods among the Indians. Not wanting to be captured by Indians or Spanish, they decided to return home.

The French may have been the first to meet the Native Americans of Michigan and begin trading with them, but soon the British wanted control of the land. Each group tried to gain Native American support. Usually, Michigan's Native Americans sided with the French. They trusted the French explorers more than the British because the French had **intermarried** with Native Americans. Native Americans also favored the French because of their generous gifts, and because they were afraid of losing their land to the British.

Unfortunately, both the British and French brought germs and diseases from Europe. The native peoples never experienced illnesses like scarlet fever, smallpox, and cholera before meeting the Europeans. When Native Americans were exposed, entire villages often became sick and died. Native Americans knew which herbs and plants to use for other illnesses, but did not know how to treat the new diseases brought by the Europeans.

Once the British realized how quickly Native Americans died from these European diseases, they deliberately infected the Native Americans. They gave blankets used by sick people to the Native Americans as gifts. It was a way of reducing the Native American population without waging battles and risking the loss of troops. If the native peoples were not there to defend their land, the explorers could easily take what they thought should be theirs.

THE BRITISH WANT TO TRADE, TOO

Tensions increased when the British decided to take control of the fur trade from the French. War broke out between the French and the British in the territories. As the war was happening here, the British and French were also at war in Europe. The European war was called the Seven Years War, lasting from 1756 to 1763.

Antoine de la Mothe Cadillac

Antoine de la Mothe Cadillac came to America in 1683 to seek his fortune. In 1694, he was placed in charge of the **fort** at Mackinac. In 1699, Cadillac went to France to get approval to create a post on the Detroit River. Cadillac believed this post would offer a better position against the invading British than Mackinac. He received land, trade privileges, and command of the new post. With a group of colonists, Detroit was founded in 1701. Cadillac also persuaded many Native Americans to settle near the new colony. When he left in 1710, his settlement was home to several thousand Native Americans.

Although there were no battles fought in the area now known as Michigan, native peoples from the area did take part in battles in other regions.

The French and Indian War began with the defeat of British General Braddock's defeat at **Fort** Duquesne in November, 1755. Native American tradition says that the Huron and Potawatomi of Michigan got their first horses as a result of this defeat. Native peoples fought on both sides during the French and Indian War, but they mainly sided with the French, which is why the war was named "the French and Indian War." The Lakes Indians were a group of Huron, Ottawa, Ojibway, and Potawatomi from the Great Lakes area who gave help to the French.

The British defeated both the French in Europe and the French and Native Americans in the colonies. The signing of the **Treaty** of Paris in 1763 officially gave the British claim to all French trading posts and forts. French soldiers and traders left the posts, but many stayed in Michigan with their families. As a result, life changed again for Michigan Native Americans and those who lived nearby.

PONTIAC REBELS

After the French and Indian War, native peoples struggled to keep their lands. There were more than 30 years of land arguments, peace treaties, and unsuccessful attempts at trying to live peacefully with the Europeans. The agreements they made never lasted. Finally, Ottawa leader Pontiac planned a great uprising. He feared his people would lose even more hunting grounds to European settlement. In 1763, Pontiac urged the tribes to come together to preserve their land. He organized tribes, including the Potawatomi, Huron, Miami, Kickapoo, Sauk, and Delaware living to the south, to rally with him against the British in Michigan and throughout the Ohio Valley. They planned attacks at each British fort following the French and Indian War. Known in history as "Pontiac's Rebellion," they overtook all but three forts.

The most difficult fight was at Fort Detroit. To succeed, Pontiac needed the help of the French who stayed in Michigan after the French and Indian War. He thought they would help by supplying **ammunition,** but they did not. Without their help, most of the other leaders **surrendered,** but Pontiac held out until 1766. From that time until his death in 1769, Pontiac promoted peace instead of fighting against the British and Americans. A member of the Kaskaskia tribe killed Pontiac near St. Louis, Missouri. Historians are not sure if his killer was paid by the British or angered because of Pontiac's change of view.

Pontiac accused the British troops of bringing infected blankets to the Native Americans in hopes of giving them deadly diseases.

As more and more settlers arrived in the colonies, native peoples saw their land being taken over by people who wanted to live there.

KING GEORGE III MAKES TROUBLE

The King's Royal Proclamation of 1763 gave American colonists another reason to not move into Michigan. After the French and Indian War, King George III tried to make peace with the native peoples living under British rule. He hoped they would not attack the British **forts** again. He **proclaimed** that pioneers were not allowed to travel westward and settle on Native American hunting grounds. The boundary he set in 1768 closed off the Ohio River Valley to settlement. This was called the **Treaty** of Fort Stanwix. Some settlers did not obey the new law. The new rule especially angered the colonists and **immigrants** who had already claimed land in this western area. Many came and settled anyway. They proved King George III and Britain could not enforce the laws they made across the ocean. The immigrants and new settlers were ready for independence.

THE REVOLUTIONARY WAR IN MICHIGAN

The Revolutionary War between the colonists and Britain began in 1775. The war did not immediately affect the Native Americans, who viewed the war as a conflict between "father and son," meaning Britain and the colonists. At first, British and American authorities also asked the Indians to not take part in any battles. However, the native peoples thought they could protect their lands if they helped the British. There were no battles fought in Michigan, but the British controlled the forts here. They had headquarters in Michigan at Fort Detroit and a new fort built on Mackinac Island, Fort Mackinac. The British location in Michigan and along the Great Lakes played an important role during the Americans' fight for independence.

British officers thought the island fort would offer better protection than old Fort Michilimackinac at the tip of the Lower Peninsula. In 1781, they moved the old fort and the buildings across the frozen strait onto Mackinac Island. They moved it section by section and rebuilt Fort Mackinac atop the hill on the island.

The Revolutionary War lasted until 1783, when the Treaty of Paris turned the British rule over to the

From the fort at Mackinac, troops could see advancing armies long before they reached the area.

Americans. The **treaty** affected Native Americans living throughout the Great Lakes, especially when the new United States borders were set. The new northern border ran right through the middle of the Great Lakes. The southern half of the lakes belonged to the U.S., and the northern half became Canada. The new borders cut through the middle of many Native American communities as well

The Northwest Ordinance of 1787 created the Northwest Territory out of land south of the Great Lakes. It included land east of the Mississippi River and north of the Ohio River to the Great Lakes. Michigan and the other future states of Indiana, Ohio, Illinois, and Wisconsin were part of this region. This territory was open for settlement. The Native American people of the region would soon see their homelands invaded by colonists. In efforts to make peace, and in hopes of saving their lands, the Native American tribes signed many treaties with the United States. However, time after time, the promises of the treaties were broken by the government.

THE BATTLE OF FALLEN TIMBERS

In 1792, President George Washington named General "Mad Anthony" Wayne as the commander of the United States Army of the Northwest,

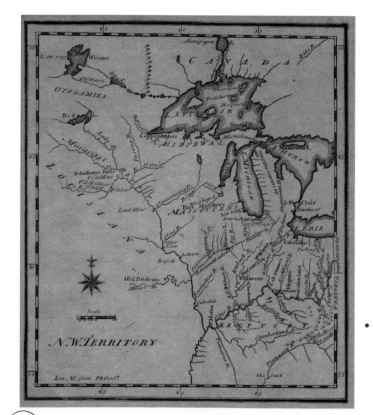

The creation of the Northwest Territory worried the native peoples of the Great Lakes area.

"Owning" the Land

Land concepts of Native American people differed greatly from that of the British and Americans. In the Native American belief system, land, like air and water, was available to all on basis of need. Personal ownership was limited to things that were made, crops raised, or what they caught while hunting and fishing. It took many years before the Native Americans realized that **ceding** land meant more than just letting other people use it.

currently serving in the Northwest Territory. The major purpose of this army was to defend American settlers from Native American attack as the army tried to take over the land. Shawnee, Miami, Delaware, Ottawa, and Ojibway Indians all participated in the battles against the U.S. Army. As Wayne and his men moved toward the Maumee River in Ohio, the Native Americans prepared to attack him at an area known as Fallen Timbers, named so because a tornado had knocked down many of the trees. Although the Native Americans used the fallen trees for cover, Wayne's men drove the Native Americans from the battlefield. The Native Amer-

The Native Americans lost the Battle of Fallen Timbers to General Anthony Wayne.

icans retreated to **Fort** Miami, hoping the British there would provide them with protection and assistance against Wayne's army. The British refused. For the next year, Wayne stayed at Fort Greenville, negotiating a **treaty** with the Native Americans. The natives realized that they were at a serious disadvantage with the Americans, especially because of Britain's refusal to support them.

Following their defeat at the Battle of Fallen Timbers in 1794, more than a thousand leaders representing a dozen Native American tribes met with Americans to sign the Treaty of Greenville in 1795. Michigan tribes sent Ojibway Chief Matchekewis to represent the Ojibway, Ottawa, and Potawatomi. The Treaty of Greenville allowed Native American people to hunt on the land until it was settled. This treaty gave way to even more American settlement. It also marked the first time that Native American tribes in Michigan signed treaties with the United States that included the exchange of rights to land occupancy.

It took over eight months to come to an agreement about the terms of the Treaty of Greenville.

After Ohio became the first state carved from the Northwest Territory in 1803, the region left was named the Indiana Territory. One year later, President Jefferson approved the Michigan Territory. Even with the new name, few settlers came to the territory.

WAR OF 1812

The American colonists were still not happy with how they were being treated by Britain. Although the colonies were in complete control of their land, Britain was still controlling the seas, forcing the colonists' ships to pay taxes whenever they tried to trade goods with other countries. The British were also moving in along the Canadian border, and this worried the colonists. Meanwhile, efforts to stop the colonists' advance into Native American territory did not entirely end with the Battle of the Fallen Timbers and the Treaty of Greenville. Tenskwatawa, also known as The Prophet, and Tecumseh, the sons of a Shawnee chief, led further resistance to the settlers advance.

Tecumseh believed in fighting the white settlers who tried to live on Native American land.

However, the native peoples were defeated by U.S. General William Henry Harrison, at Tippecanoe, Indiana, in 1811. General Harrison feared the strength of the native peoples group led by Tecumseh and his brother, and wanted to stop it. The Battle of Tippecanoe on November 7, 1811, began a new round of fighting between the native peoples and the colonists. These events led to Native American participation in the War of 1812.

The first battles of the war occurred in 1813. The United States hoped to invade Canada, but Britain successfully held off the troops. The U.S. did have two important victories. One was at the Battle of Lake Erie, giving the United States control of that Great Lake. The other was the Battle of the Thames, where General Harrison defeated a combined British and Native American force led by Henry Procter and Tecumseh. Tecumseh died during the battle.

In 1814, the war turned against the Americans. A British army captured and held Washington, D.C., for a brief period. Before the British **evacuated** the city, they set

After Tecumseh's death, most of the remaining warriors lost hope and left the battlefield.

fire to several of the buildings, including the White House. By late 1814, both the Americans and the British were ready to end the war. The two sides signed the **Treaty** of Ghent on December 24, 1814. Before news of the peace treaty reached the soldiers in the U.S., the Battle of New Orleans took place in January, 1815.

NATIVE AMERICAN REMOVAL

For the rest of the Native Americans in Michigan, the following years led them on a painful journey. The American government asked the native peoples to sign more treaties. They were called cession treaties because the Native Americans were forced to **cede** their lands to the government. The U.S. government paid a small amount of money for these large pieces of land and allowed the tribes to hunt on the land until it was settled. In 1819, Governor Cass of the Michigan Territory arranged the Treaty of Saginaw. This resulted in Ojibway tribes ceding their villages and hunting grounds, which covered nearly half of the Lower Peninsula.

In Michigan, some tribes were given a reserve, or a small area of land, when they signed treaties. President Andrew Jackson did not like the idea of reserves. He wanted all the Michigan native peoples moved west of the Mississippi River. President Jackson thought they were interfering with American settlement. Many Native American people on the reserves in the Michigan Territory left their homes by the time Michigan became a state on January 26, 1837. They moved north into the Upper Peninsula and Canada, or west to Wisconsin and Minnesota.

Most Michigan tribes lost all but a very small portion of their **vast** farmlands while signing treaties with the U.S. government. Potawatomi chief Leopold Pokagon did not want to leave Michigan with the others. He and his followers stayed. They helped build a Catholic **mission** along the St. Joseph River and became Catholic farmers.

In 1840, President Jackson sent General Hugh Brady to remove any remaining Native Americans from Michigan. This did not happen easily. There were no battles over the land, but the Indians would not just pack up and leave either. It took many years and many complicated treaties to decide what land belonged to whom and where Michigan's native peoples could live. This uncertainty lasted more than thirty years until the Dawes Act in 1887 settled how reservation lands would be parceled out. This act was unsuccessful, however, as many native peoples refused to leave their land in Michigan.

Chief Pokagon

Michigan Indians Today

Many native peoples have returned to Michigan since the days of Native American removal. Many who make their home here have **ancestors** from different tribes. Most of the native peoples in Michigan belong to the Anishinaabe Three Fires Confederacy. Some can trace their ancestry to the tribes that were in Michigan in the past. Others share family trees with tribes from other parts of the U.S. According to the 2000 U.S. Census, about 60,000 Michigan residents are Native Americans.

Modern powwows are based upon ancient traditions of tribal gatherings that feature dance, music, storytelling, and ceremonies.

Michigan Tribes

Michigan's twelve federally-recognized tribes:

Bay Mills Chippewa Indian Community

Grand Traverse Bay Band of Ottawa and Chippewa Indians

Hannahville Potawatomi Indian Community

Huron Potawatomi-Nottawaseppi Huron Band of Potawatomi

Keweenaw Bay Indian Community

Lac Vieux Desert Band of Lake Superior Chippewa Indians

Little River Band of Odawa Indians

Little Traverse Bay Band of Odawa Indians

Match-e-be-nash-she-wish Band of Potawatomi Indians of Michigan

Pokagon Band of Potawatomi Indians

Saginaw Chippewa Indian Tribe

Sault Ste. Marie Tribe of Chippewa Indians

Michigan's three state-recognized tribes:

Grand River Bands of Ottawa Indians

Burt Lake Band of Ottawa and Chippewa Indians

Swan Creek/Black River Confederated Ojibway Tribes of Michigan

NATIVE AMERICANS ON RESERVATIONS AND IN MICHIGAN COMMUNITIES

There are 12 federally-recognized tribes in Michigan and 3 state-recognized tribes. Thousands of native peoples live on these reservations, but many more are members who live in communities throughout Michigan. There are also many bands of native peoples that are not federally recognized. That is, they live in Michigan, but do not have reservation lands that receive support and protection from the federal government.

Many native peoples whose ancestors belonged to other tribes throughout the United States came to Michigan to find better jobs. During the Industrial Revolution, beginning around 1860, they moved to Michigan along with others who wanted high-paying factory jobs in Michigan's automotive **industry.** Today,

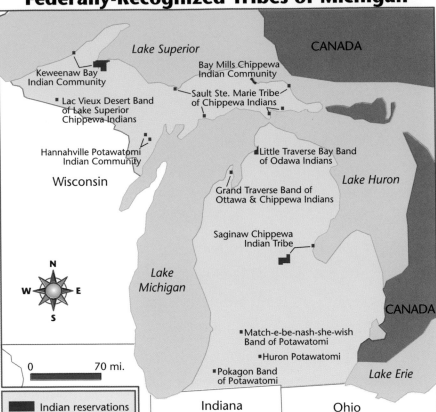

Federally-Recognized Tribes of Michigan

Lake Superior

CANADA

Keweenaw Bay
Indian Community

Bay Mills Chippewa
Indian Community

Lac Vieux Desert Band
of Lake Superior
Chippewa Indians

Sault Ste. Marie Tribe
of Chippewa Indians

Hannahville Potawatomi
Indian Community

Little Traverse Bay Band
of Odawa Indians

Wisconsin

Lake Huron

Grand Traverse Band of
Ottawa & Chippewa Indians

Saginaw Chippewa
Indian Tribe

Lake
Michigan

CANADA

Match-e-be-nash-she-wish
Band of Potawatomi

Huron Potawatomi

0   70 mi.

Pokagon Band
of Potawatomi

Lake Erie

Indian reservations

Indiana

Ohio

Being a federally-recognized tribe means that the U.S. government acknowledges that the tribes have the right to govern the land on which the tribal members live and work.

many Native Americans live in cities and communities throughout Michigan and have **occupations** just like other residents. Some Native Americans prefer the work of their **ancestors**—hunting and fishing. Others operate or work in **casinos** within the boundaries of their reservations.

One example of a modern Michigan Native American community is in Wilson. The Hannahville Indian Community of Michigan is home to about 470 of its 700 tribal members. Most of the remaining members live in surrounding communities. The federal government recognizes Hannahville as a Potawatomi tribal community. This Potawatomi tribe has a **treaty** relationship with the U.S. government. Like other tribes who are eager to teach their **culture** to their youngsters, the Potawatomi hold an annual powwow each summer. Thousands of Native Americans from all over the United States gather to share their customs and retell their stories.

Life as a Michigan Native American

Dan Shepard is an Ottawa who lives at Little River Band Ottawa Indians in Manistee. "Our tribal land was reaffirmed in 1994. It was like a checkerboard, with bits and pieces of land. We are developing a fire station, school, water treatment facility, housing, and insurance—everything you need for a community. There are families who live here and more that are moving back. We have our own **judicial** system and work with the government. We are like a state." Mr. Shepard's job is issuing land and building permits. When there is a death in the tribe, his job is also the "firekeeper," carrying out tribal traditions.

Mr. Shepard says he can trace his ancestors back to two tribal chiefs who signed a treaty with the government in 1836, a year before Michigan became a state. He says about one of every four people in his community work at the casino on the reservation. He and his people are learning the language and customs that were forgotten. "It is a difficult language to learn because is unique—there is not another like it and some meanings have four different words. We have a special language camp. Families come to study our language," he explained.

NATIVE AMERICAN SCHOOLS

After the native peoples lost their land to the U.S. government, schools were set up to try to make Native Americans **assimilate** and become **Christians. Missionaries** ran most Native American schools, and many were located in or very near the church building. Teachers at Indian schools were both Native American and white, but they were all Christian. Native American schools rarely had enough money to pay their teachers well, so experienced teachers often got jobs elsewhere. Native American teachers often could not get jobs elsewhere, so they frequently taught at Native American schools.

Both native and white students attended Indian schools. The white children were mostly the children of

missionaries and a few white settlers who lived around the mission. Students often had no paper or pencils and schools were not always heated.

The Mt. Pleasant Indian **Boarding School** was open from 1891 until 1934. Historical records show that some students referred to the school as the "Mt. Pleasant Indian Jail." Being away from family members was very difficult for students who were used to their close tribal community. The school rules demanded that students wear uniforms, respond to bell signals, and spend half their day in class and the other half doing chores such as growing crops and caring for animals. This system was uncomfortable for students who were used to traditional Native American ways of living and learning.

Holy Childhood Catholic School is no longer open, but the nearby Catholic church remains active.

After the Mt. Pleasant Indian Boarding School closed in 1934, most Native American students were forced to attend public schools.

Holy Childhood Catholic School in Harbor Springs was opened in 1829. It was both a day and boarding school. The school was run in much the same way as the Mt. Pleasant Indian Boarding School. Towards the end of its operation, however, students were encouraged to maintain their **heritage** by speaking their tribal languages, making traditional crafts, and participating in celebrations.

Today, Native American children growing up in Michigan have the opportunity to learn more about their ancestry and traditions of their tribes. Besides learning about these things from their families, there are several schools in Michigan that are run by different tribes. The Binoojiinh Montessori school in Saginaw is part of the Saginaw Chippewa Indian Tribe. Students at this school learn the same subjects as those attending public schools, but they also learn about their **heritage,** including the Anishinaabe language, storytelling, crafts, and traditional food preparation. Each year the school hosts a traditional powwow that brings together students from area schools and features its own students as dancers and workers.

The Nahtahwahsh School, which means Soaring Eagle, was originally opened by the Hannahville Indian Tribe to serve Potawatomi students. Today, students of any **ethnicity** can attend. This school was the first tribally-controlled school in the state of Michigan. Other schools include Bahweting Anishnabe School which has been

Native American Influence

run by the Sault Ste. Marie Tribe of Chippewa Indians since 1994. The Grand Traverse Band of Ottawa and Chippewa Tribes has a school as well.

A LASTING INFLUENCE

Native American communities throughout the Upper and Lower Peninsulas left their mark on Michigan. Native American words and ideas are shared everyday in Michigan. Members of Native American tribes live, work, and play in a state that was home to their **ancestors** many years ago. They are proud of their heritage and connection to the land. The **descendants** of Michigan's native peoples are working to keep their traditions alive for many generations to come.

Native American Counties

Many names in Michigan have Native American roots. Here are a few Michigan counties with Native American names.

Newaygo: named after an Ottawa chief

Mecosta: comes from the Ojibway word meaning "bear"

Muskegon: comes from the Ojibway word for "swamp" or "marsh"

Saginaw: comes from the Ojibway word for outlet of a river

Genesee: comes from an Iroquoian word meaning "beautiful valley"

Sanilac: named after a Huron chief

Chippewa: French name for the Ojibway tribe

Kalamazoo: may mean "boiling water," "otter tail," or "reflected river"

Ottawa: named for the Ottawa tribe called "Ondatahouats," or "people of the forest," by the Hurons

Map of Michigan

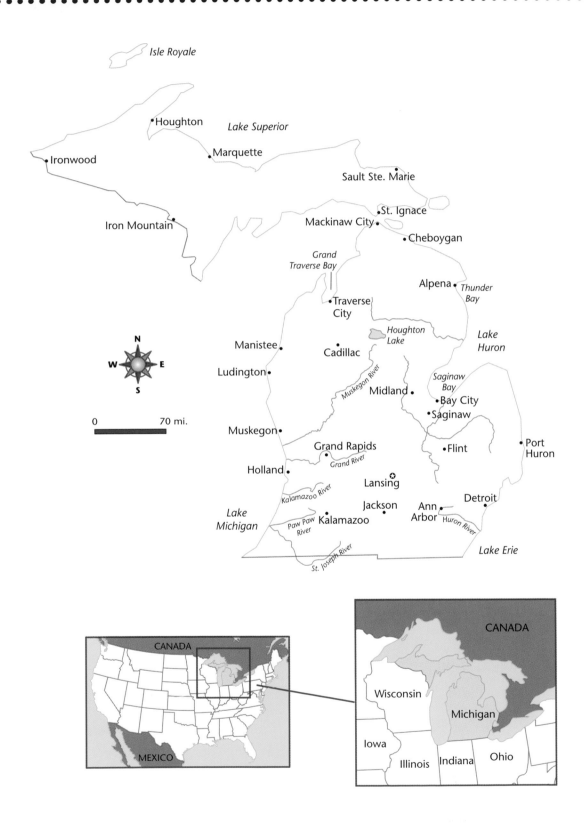

Isle Royale

•Houghton   Lake Superior

Ironwood

•Marquette

Sault Ste. Marie

Iron Mountain

St. Ignace

Mackinaw City•

•Cheboygan

Grand
Traverse Bay

Alpena•   Thunder
            Bay

•Traverse
  City

Houghton
Lake

Lake
Huron

N
W   E
S

Manistee

Cadillac

Saginaw
Bay

Ludington

Muskegon River

Midland

•Bay City

•Saginaw

0   70 mi.

Muskegon

Grand Rapids

Grand River

•Flint

Port
Huron

Holland

Lansing

Kalamazoo River

Jackson

Ann
Arbor

Detroit

Lake
Michigan

Paw Paw
River

Kalamazoo

Huron River

St. Joseph River

Lake Erie

CANADA

CANADA

Wisconsin

Michigan

MEXICO

Iowa

Illinois   Indiana   Ohio

44

Timeline

20,000 B.C.E.	Earliest people arrive on the **continent** of North America.
8,000–500 B.C.E.	Last **Ice Age** ends and the Archaic people arrive. Old Copper Indians mine copper.
500 B.C.E.	Woodland peoples come to the area. The early moundbuilders known as the Hopewell Indians settle.
About 1600 C.E.	Three Fires Tribes—Ojibway, Ottawa, and Potawatomi—**migrate** to the area now known as Michigan.
About 1620	French explorers arrive in the Great Lakes area. They set up trading posts and **missions.**
1701	**Fort** Pontchartrain du De Troit (Detroit) founded.
1735	The French and Indian War begins.
1763	France loses all its land rights in America after losing the French and Indian War and signing the **Treaty** of Paris. Pontiac's Rebellion takes place.
1768	Treaty of Stanwix signed. This treaty declared all land west of the Ohio River to be for Native American settlement only.
1775–1783	The Revolutionary War takes place.
1787	Northwest Ordinance passed.
1794	Treaty of Greenville signed. This treaty allowed native peoples to hunt on the land until it was settled.
1805	Michigan Territory created with its first **capital** in Detroit.
1811	Battle of Tippecanoe takes place. This began further fighting between the Native Americans and the colonists.
1812	Fort Mackinac and Fort Detroit are **surrendered** by the British.
1819	Treaty of Saginaw signed. This treaty led to Ojibway tribes **ceding** all of their land to the government.
1829	Holy Childhood day and **boarding school** opens in Harbor Springs.
1837	Michigan becomes 26th state with a capital in Detroit and Stevens Mason as first governor.
1887	Dawes Act of 1887 passed. This act determined how reservations would be parceled out.
1891	Mt. Pleasant Boarding School opens.

Glossary

agriculture having to do with farming

Algonquian group of Native American languages spoken by many native peoples living in Canada, New England, and the Great Lakes region

ammunition objects fired from guns or used in war

ancestor one from whom an individual has descended

archaeologist person who studies history through the remains of people and what they have made or built

archaic related to an early period of time

artifact something created by humans for a practical purpose during a certain time period

assimilate take something in and make it part of what it has joined

boarding school school at which most students live during the school year

capital location of a government

casino building used for entertainments such as card games

cede give up because of an agreement made between two groups

Christian person who believes in the teachings of Jesus. They follow a religion called Christianity.

clan group of people who share a common relative who lived in the past

climate weather conditions that are usual for a certain area

continent one of the great divisions of land on the globe; Asia, Antarctica, Australia, Africa, Europe, North America, and South America are the seven continents of the world

culture ideas, skills, arts, and a way of life of a certain people of a certain time

descend come from a person whose family background can be traced to a certain individual or group

dialect form of language belonging to a certain region

economy control of money that is earned and spent in a home, business, or government

evacuate force everyone in a certain area to leave

expedition organized journey of a group of people

foraging searching for food

fort strong building used for defense against enemy attack

game animal hunted for food or sport

heritage something that comes from one's ancestors

hostile angry and unfriendly

humanity all humans

humility being humble and not proud

Ice Age period of colder climate when much of North America was covered by thick glaciers

immigrant one who moves to another country to settle

industry group of businesses that offer a similar product or service

inherit to get by legal right from a person after his or her death

intermarry marriage between two people of different groups

interpret tell the meaning of

judicial branch of government that explains or interprets the laws of the state or nation

mammoth large, extinct animal, similar to an elephant, with shaggy hair and long tusks

mastodon large, extinct animal, similar to an elephant but smaller than a mammoth, with shaggy hair and long tusks

maturity being fully grown into an adult

migrate move from one place to another for food or work

missionary person sent by a church to spread his or her religious beliefs; a mission is a place where missionaries live and work.

mixed-ancestry having a family background from several different groups

moccasin shoe made of soft leather made from deer skins

nomadic moving from place to place following herds of wild animals

occupation type of employment

pelt skin taken from an animal

petroglyph ancient carving on rock

prehistoric from the time before history was written

proclaim announce publicly

remnant something that remains or is left over

subsistence what is necessary to continue living, such as food and water

surrender give oneself or something over to the power, control, or possession of someone else

tanning process by which an animal hide is scraped, soaked, and washed

treaty agreement reached between two or more groups

vast very large in size or amount

More Books to Read

Benton-Benai, Edward. *The Mishomis Book*. Hayward, Wisc.: Indian Country Communications, Incorporated, 1988.

Gibson, Karen Bush. *The Potawatomi*. Minnetonka, Minn.: Capstone Press, 2002.

Landau, Elaine. *The Ottawa*. Danbury, Conn.: Scholastic Library Publishing, 2000.

Schmittroth, Felkins Ryan. *Ojibway*. Farmington Hills, Mich.: Gale Group, 2003.

Williams, Suzanne. *Ojibwe Indians*. Chicago: Heinemann Library, 2003.

Index

About the Author

Award-winning photographer and journalist Marcia Schonberg is the author of travel guides, nonfiction children's books, and the Heinemann Library Ohio State Studies books. She has contributed to *Michigan Living* and writes regularly for daily newspapers and regional and national magazines. A mother of three, Marcia resides in the Midwest with her husband Bill and golden retriever, Cassie.